CHECK REGISTER BOOK

Name: _______________

Phone: _______________

Check Register Book

Date Range

No.	Date	Description	Ref	Debit	Credit	Balance

Check Register Book

Date Range

No.	Date	Description	Ref	Debit	Credit	Balance

Check Register Book

No.	Date	Description	Ref	Debit	Credit	Balance

Check Register Book

Date Range

No.	Date	Description	Ref	Debit	Credit	Balance

Check Register Book

Date Range

No.	Date	Description	Ref	Debit	Credit	Balance

Check Register Book

No.	Date	Description	Ref	Debit	Credit	Balance

Check Register Book

No.	Date	Description	Ref	Debit	Credit	Balance

Check Register Book

Date Range

No.	Date	Description	Ref	Debit	Credit	Balance

Check Register Book

Date Range

No.	Date	Description	Ref	Debit	Credit	Balance

Check Register Book

Date Range

No.	Date	Description	Ref	Debit	Credit	Balance

Check Register Book

No.	Date	Description	Ref	Debit	Credit	Balance

Check Register Book

Date Range

No.	Date	Description	Ref	Debit	Credit	Balance

Check Register Book

Date Range

No.	Date	Description	Ref	Debit	Credit	Balance

Check Register Book

Date Range

No.	Date	Description	Ref	Debit	Credit	Balance

Check Register Book

No.	Date	Description	Ref	Debit	Credit	Balance

Check Register Book

Date Range

No.	Date	Description	Ref	Debit	Credit	Balance

Check Register Book

No.	Date	Description	Ref	Debit	Credit	Balance

Check Register Book

Date Range

No.	Date	Description	Ref	Debit	Credit	Balance

Check Register Book

Date Range

No.	Date	Description	Ref	Debit	Credit	Balance

Check Register Book

Date Range

No.	Date	Description	Ref	Debit	Credit	Balance

Check Register Book

Date Range

No.	Date	Description	Ref	Debit	Credit	Balance

Check Register Book

Date Range

No.	Date	Description	Ref	Debit	Credit	Balance

Check Register Book

No.	Date	Description	Ref	Debit	Credit	Balance

Check Register Book

Date Range

No.	Date	Description	Ref	Debit	Credit	Balance

Check Register Book

Date Range

No.	Date	Description	Ref	Debit	Credit	Balance

Check Register Book

No.	Date	Description	Ref	Debit	Credit	Balance

Check Register Book

No.	Date	Description	Ref	Debit	Credit	Balance

Check Register Book

No.	Date	Description	Ref	Debit	Credit	Balance

Check Register Book

No.	Date	Description	Ref	Debit	Credit	Balance

Check Register Book

Date Range

No.	Date	Description	Ref	Debit	Credit	Balance

Check Register Book

Date Range

No.	Date	Description	Ref	Debit	Credit	Balance

Check Register Book

No.	Date	Description	Ref	Debit	Credit	Balance

Check Register Book

No.	Date	Description	Ref	Debit	Credit	Balance

Check Register Book

Date Range

No.	Date	Description	Ref	Debit	Credit	Balance

Check Register Book

No.	Date	Description	Ref	Debit	Credit	Balance

Check Register Book

Date Range

No.	Date	Description	Ref	Debit	Credit	Balance

Check Register Book

Date Range

No.	Date	Description	Ref	Debit	Credit	Balance

Check Register Book

Date Range

No.	Date	Description	Ref	Debit	Credit	Balance

Check Register Book

Date Range

No.	Date	Description	Ref	Debit	Credit	Balance

Check Register Book

Date Range

No.	Date	Description	Ref	Debit	Credit	Balance

Check Register Book

Date Range

No.	Date	Description	Ref	Debit	Credit	Balance

Check Register Book

Date Range

No.	Date	Description	Ref	Debit	Credit	Balance

Check Register Book

No.	Date	Description	Ref	Debit	Credit	Balance

Check Register Book

No.	Date	Description	Ref	Debit	Credit	Balance

Check Register Book

No.	Date	Description	Ref	Debit	Credit	Balance

Check Register Book

Date Range

No.	Date	Description	Ref	Debit	Credit	Balance

Check Register Book

Date Range

No.	Date	Description	Ref	Debit	Credit	Balance

Check Register Book

No.	Date	Description	Ref	Debit	Credit	Balance

Check Register Book

No.	Date	Description	Ref	Debit	Credit	Balance

Check Register Book

Date Range

No.	Date	Description	Ref	Debit	Credit	Balance

Check Register Book

Date Range

No.	Date	Description	Ref	Debit	Credit	Balance

Check Register Book

No.	Date	Description	Ref	Debit	Credit	Balance

Check Register Book

No.	Date	Description	Ref	Debit	Credit	Balance

Check Register Book

Date Range

No.	Date	Description	Ref	Debit	Credit	Balance

Check Register Book

Date Range

No.	Date	Description	Ref	Debit	Credit	Balance

Check Register Book

Date Range

No.	Date	Description	Ref	Debit	Credit	Balance

Check Register Book

No.	Date	Description	Ref	Debit	Credit	Balance

Check Register Book

No.	Date	Description	Ref	Debit	Credit	Balance

Check Register Book

Date Range

No.	Date	Description	Ref	Debit	Credit	Balance

Check Register Book

Date Range

No.	Date	Description	Ref	Debit	Credit	Balance

Check Register Book

Date Range

No.	Date	Description	Ref	Debit	Credit	Balance

Check Register Book

Date Range

No.	Date	Description	Ref	Debit	Credit	Balance

Check Register Book

Date Range

No.	Date	Description	Ref	Debit	Credit	Balance

Check Register Book

Date Range

No.	Date	Description	Ref	Debit	Credit	Balance

Check Register Book

Date Range

No.	Date	Description	Ref	Debit	Credit	Balance

Check Register Book

Date Range

No.	Date	Description	Ref	Debit	Credit	Balance

Check Register Book

Date Range

No.	Date	Description	Ref	Debit	Credit	Balance

Check Register Book

No.	Date	Description	Ref	Debit	Credit	Balance

Check Register Book

No.	Date	Description	Ref	Debit	Credit	Balance

Check Register Book

No.	Date	Description	Ref	Debit	Credit	Balance

Check Register Book

Date Range

No.	Date	Description	Ref	Debit	Credit	Balance

Check Register Book

No.	Date	Description	Ref	Debit	Credit	Balance

Check Register Book

No.	Date	Description	Ref	Debit	Credit	Balance

Check Register Book

Date Range

No.	Date	Description	Ref	Debit	Credit	Balance

Check Register Book

No.	Date	Description	Ref	Debit	Credit	Balance

Check Register Book

Date Range

No.	Date	Description	Ref	Debit	Credit	Balance

Check Register Book

No.	Date	Description	Ref	Debit	Credit	Balance

Check Register Book

Date Range

No.	Date	Description	Ref	Debit	Credit	Balance

Check Register Book

Date Range

No.	Date	Description	Ref	Debit	Credit	Balance

Check Register Book

No.	Date	Description	Ref	Debit	Credit	Balance

Check Register Book

Date Range

No.	Date	Description	Ref	Debit	Credit	Balance

Check Register Book

Date Range

No.	Date	Description	Ref	Debit	Credit	Balance

Check Register Book

Date Range

No.	Date	Description	Ref	Debit	Credit	Balance

Check Register Book

No.	Date	Description	Ref	Debit	Credit	Balance

Check Register Book

No.	Date	Description	Ref	Debit	Credit	Balance

Check Register Book

No.	Date	Description	Ref	Debit	Credit	Balance

Check Register Book

No.	Date	Description	Ref	Debit	Credit	Balance

Check Register Book

Date Range

No.	Date	Description	Ref	Debit	Credit	Balance

Check Register Book

No.	Date	Description	Ref	Debit	Credit	Balance

Check Register Book

No.	Date	Description	Ref	Debit	Credit	Balance

Check Register Book

Date Range

No.	Date	Description	Ref	Debit	Credit	Balance

Check Register Book

No.	Date	Description	Ref	Debit	Credit	Balance

Check Register Book

No.	Date	Description	Ref	Debit	Credit	Balance

Check Register Book

Date Range

No.	Date	Description	Ref	Debit	Credit	Balance

Check Register Book

Date Range

No.	Date	Description	Ref	Debit	Credit	Balance

Check Register Book

Date Range

No.	Date	Description	Ref	Debit	Credit	Balance

Check Register Book

No.	Date	Description	Ref	Debit	Credit	Balance

Check Register Book

Date Range

No.	Date	Description	Ref	Debit	Credit	Balance

Check Register Book

No.	Date	Description	Ref	Debit	Credit	Balance

Check Register Book

Date Range

No.	Date	Description	Ref	Debit	Credit	Balance

Check Register Book

No.	Date	Description	Ref	Debit	Credit	Balance

Check Register Book

Date Range

No.	Date	Description	Ref	Debit	Credit	Balance

Check Register Book

Date Range

No.	Date	Description	Ref	Debit	Credit	Balance

Check Register Book

Date Range

No.	Date	Description	Ref	Debit	Credit	Balance

Check Register Book

Date Range

No.	Date	Description	Ref	Debit	Credit	Balance

Check Register Book

No.	Date	Description	Ref	Debit	Credit	Balance

Check Register Book

Date Range

No.	Date	Description	Ref	Debit	Credit	Balance

Check Register Book

Date Range

No.	Date	Description	Ref	Debit	Credit	Balance

Check Register Book

No.	Date	Description	Ref	Debit	Credit	Balance

Check Register Book

Date Range

No.	Date	Description	Ref	Debit	Credit	Balance

Check Register Book

No.	Date	Description	Ref	Debit	Credit	Balance

Check Register Book

Date Range

No.	Date	Description	Ref	Debit	Credit	Balance

Check Register Book

No.	Date	Description	Ref	Debit	Credit	Balance

Check Register Book

Date Range

No.	Date	Description	Ref	Debit	Credit	Balance

Check Register Book

No.	Date	Description	Ref	Debit	Credit	Balance

Check Register Book

Date Range

No.	Date	Description	Ref	Debit	Credit	Balance

Check Register Book

Date Range

No.	Date	Description	Ref	Debit	Credit	Balance

Check Register Book

Date Range

No.	Date	Description	Ref	Debit	Credit	Balance

Check Register Book

Date Range

No.	Date	Description	Ref	Debit	Credit	Balance